Borderlands

poems by

Margaret Adams Birth

Finishing Line Press
Georgetown, Kentucky

Borderlands

Copyright © 2016 by Margaret Adams Birth
ISBN 978-1-944251-51-2 First Edition
All rights reserved under International and Pan-American Copyright Conventions.
No part of this book may be reproduced in any manner whatsoever without written permission from the publisher, except in the case of brief quotations embodied in critical articles and reviews.

ACKNOWLEDGMENTS

I thank these publications where the following poems from this collection have previously appeared, sometimes in different forms:

"Ancient Lullabies" in *Burningword Literary Journal*
"East-southeast" in *The Wild Goose Poetry Review*
"Freedom of Release" in *Ship of Fools*
"My Friend Persimmon" in *Aura Literary/Arts Review*
"One coldgray Pickle-morning" in *Black River Review*
"The Prospect (Park) of a Perfect Summer Day" in *Atlantic Pacific Press*
"Springtime on Stage" in *Blue Lake Review*

Editor: Christen Kincaid

Cover Art: © 2014, Margaret Adams Birth

Author Photo: Brendan Birth

Cover Design: Elizabeth Maines

Printed in the USA on acid-free paper.
Order online: www.finishinglinepress.com
　　　　　also available on amazon.com

Author inquiries and mail orders:
Finishing Line Press
P. O. Box 1626
Georgetown, Kentucky 40324
U. S. A.

Table of Contents

An Explanation: Borders versus Borderlands 1

Ancient Lullabies 2

East-southeast 3

Granddaddy 4

Sunrise at Miller's Pond 5

Sister Acedia 6

One coldgray Pickle-morning 7

Freedom of Release 8

The Beggar on 32nd Street 9

Southern Paradox 11

Dreaming without Feeling 13

Lot's Wife, Revised and Updated for a New Millennium 15

Farewell Father 16

Springtime on Stage 17

Practicing Therapy 18

My Friend Persimmon 19

Monkey Business 20

Revelation 21

The Radiant Point 22

The Prospect (Park) of a Perfect Summer Day 23

Reunion 25

Reflections 26

The Other Side 27

*To my husband, Kevin Birth,
and to our sons, Brendan and Aidan,
with deepest love*

Borders versus Borderlands

A border is a line, a boundary, a set edge of territory within which one place, or state of being, or feeling is defined and outside of which another is defined; the poems in this collection are not about strict borders.

These poems, instead, are about borderlands: those often-fuzzy, indefinable regions that are between borders or that are in near-but-not-quite-to-the-edges areas approaching borders. The poems in this collection explore a variety of borderlands—sometimes physical places, sometimes spiritual explorations or revelations, sometimes based in reality but at other times simply inspired by fascination with an image or a set of sounds, or sometimes something else as fuzzy and indefinable as borderlands themselves.

Front cover photograph:
"From Lindisfarne to St. Cuthbert's Isle," © 2014, Margaret Adams Birth

This picture depicts a borderland of a sort: Lindisfarne, also known as Holy Island, is a tidal island in England—meaning that, at low tide, there are rocky or muddy areas between it and the mainland, as well as between it and nearby St. Cuthbert's Isle, which can be crossed on foot or (in certain spots) by car, but at high tide, Lindisfarne and St. Cuthbert's are surrounded by water and are not easily accessible. It was because of this relative isolation that the area held an appeal to early Celtic Christians—not only to St. Cuthbert, but also to St. Eadfrith, St. Eadberht and St. Aidan, among others.

Ancient Lullabies

1

Dew-wet grass glistens under pink morning sun,
and a bee, that liberated prophetess of old,
now silently hovers in the air above, conceiving
of all the truths that are yet to be told.

2

The full-grown, ripened tranquility lingers
where honeysuckle spills over and blankets
one section of rusty wire fence, half-fallen
to the ground; the grass softly sighs.

3

The time of longer days has bared its noon,
refined, haze-hot whiteness languorously awaiting a silver moon
that sits high on a coral horizon: Don't
try to sketch an outline, but let it paint itself.

4

Empty lots: July's saccharine kudzu chokes all
that's in its path as afternoon thunderstorms
spur the vines on to wilder and yet more
uncontrollable growth; autumn will halt the onslaught.

5

Choruses of ancient lullabies wait in shadows
here, where childhood secrets and open sky
declaim in verse, unsung yet clear, the stories
learned by Devorah when summer's grass blades bent low.

East-southeast

She believed it was in Georgia—that spot
which lay far-distant, like a dot of mossy green
rhythmically slicing to and fro across the back
of her closed eye, like a platinum scimitar standing
guard over Taurus and Orion, like a concave-cut piece of glass
revealing every visible thing but revealing it
shrunken in minute perfection.

Dusty thickets of cotton and rice genuflected to
the coastal breeze, received summer's humid
baptism and the holy kisses of mosquito and bee,
where the land met the Atlantic, and the blessings
of this place did not seem immediately clear.
The ocean glistened flatly, barren of autumn's swells,
and reflected life forms scraping the shallow line
between brackish water and salty sand.

But even a cardinal can recall where
last it built its nest, and the fields, and the pines
and the weeping willows that trace the saffron sunlight and
the puckish shadows, acting as a natural compass to *there*;
you would think that some tint, some scent would linger
in her brain, some hint of place or name—
and yet, she was just as lost in fantasy as she was in real life.

Too much familiarity could prove nothing but bad, she had
once thought: A bleeding heart could be a flower or a sympathizer,
and she had picked the former—to watch the world fly by;
but insanity mocked reality, and then all she could do was lie
abed dreaming of towers of clouds and dancing bulls,
of golden insects and red-hot sunsets, and of all the details
belonging to that one spot she would have
wished to call her own.

Granddaddy

I still see him as he looked
in later years—liver spots and keratoses covering
his skin, his hair
white (the combination of all colors,
the reflection of all frequencies of colors
in the spectrum); in his eyes,
the bright silver-blue of an antique mirror,
I glimpse his daughter, my mother, his near-image;
I see the same shade in her gaze today,
only she's already over a decade older
than he when the tobacco, and asphalt and asbestos
caught up with his muscles and lungs.

A mystery since before the age of twenty-five—
or was it twenty-nine?—he was born
in Florida, or Georgia (Decatur city? Or county? Or maybe Weston?),
   or Alabama,
named Jack, or Jackson A., or Jackson C., or John Thomas, or
   Jonathan;
he made his history his story alone—
was his mother a Dismuke or a Patterson,
his father an Adams, an Adom, an Adonis, or a Sims,
his uncle a country doctor, his mother and sister killed in a house fire,
and did the fire orphan him, or did his father abandon him?
Did he believe in any of the characters he playacted
for my mother, or did a bit of each exist in his true character—
a character that reflected all the frequencies that combined in the
   spectrum of his life?

Sunrise at Miller's Pond

A miasma of morning fog
obscures the air above the pond—approach with care;
scarlet rays of dawn on the horizon
shimmer—almost slither—
as they try to break through and burn off
the near-opaque atmosphere.
Is it still as picture-perfect as you recalled?
Halt halfway down the hill that leads to water's edge
and see a stand of coreopsis that glows with showy golden blooms—
it serves as a vivid monument to verdant life beside
the marshy ground. The murky vapor
shrinks, slowly but perceptibly, as the sun rises higher in the sky,
and you can't help but think of a warning you once heard:
that "nothing is hidden that will not be disclosed."

Sister Acedia

On a morning when hope should shine in its chill light,
she is singing a sad song that keens
through the green buds blooming,

through the pollen-laced grass of the spring garden
beyond her window. She is plodding through her sunshine-yellow
kitchen on a morning she wishes were filled with hope.

She is grinding the coffee and cooking on the stove.
And she is mourning as she moves through the motions
of her day in a home where no one else lives.

Once, she would have danced through the musical light
with shadows following her in the sweet air
of a morning with hope. But today she is singing

a song that overwhelms even the blues, that is true dirge,
as she shuffles through the home where she
is weeping, wailing that her song

provides no better expression of misery than any other tune.
Sinners may yet boast about their good fortune,
but she believes it wisest to prepare for the worst.

One coldgray Pickle-morning

      One coldgray Pickle-morning sitI
        Knittingona Purple-thing . . .
           Raveling
             and
                      unravelingit
asI
        Ravel-andunravel
                          The
                       questions-the
            Answersihavein my
mind:

Freedom of Release

She exits the cave of a dark new-moon night, thinking that it feels
   like her moans will
continue echoing—though they're now so tremulous she wonders if
   others could hear
the last of them released in her sense of morning-light relief. Last
   night
they slowly built until they reverberated
within her chest. Could anyone comprehend the degree of pain
deflected by the relief she feels as she lifts the shades at break of
   dawn?
It's the first day of spring, and she walks five miles
through the city, watching buildings sprout from piles of melting
   snow.
Afterward, she dares to quiz one or two close friends:
Do you ever journey through the winter pain within your soul?
The ache is a solid something that pounds the heart relentlessly, she
   says,
swelling it to overflowing discomfort—could this be my be-
ing, alone? In this, too, am I solitary and alone?
When the pain encounters the relief of new-season daylight,
it feels as if she floats, a cloud suddenly bursting bright within her
   chest,
and though she doesn't understand, she attempts to accept
the freedom of release within the open sky.

The Beggar on 32nd Street

Back against the concrete wall of a building on
32nd Street, the man with a bushy, scruffy beard
lays hands in lap, palms open, making an anemic-
looking effort at begging, as if to say, simply,

"I'm empty." He holds no used coffee cup with coins
placed in the bottom to rattle his need to the world,
as other street-beggars do; he makes no
snake-oil-salesman pitch about some bogus charity, either—

that's the subway-beggars' way; this man just sits in an out-of-the-way
doorway, looking like one of St. Francis's original Assisi
mendicant brothers, or maybe a meditating Gandhi
transported from India to Midtown.

I could reach into my purse, I know,
pull out pennies, nickels, quarters, dimes, even a dollar or
two, then shove them at him and keep moving;
I could give my righteous alms and still promptly make my meeting.

I could do it almost without thinking, easily without feeling;
I could leave him quickly, both of us as comfortable as when I'd
     arrived—
not considering the man, not confronting my own motive,
not caring what my actions might suggest about his nature . . . or
     mine.

I'm not sure he'd even miss me if I walked straight past;
he could assume that I'm just another clueless tourist,
     staring upward, toward the Empire State Building, not noticing where
     I go.
He'd never have to know how I grappled with heart and head.

"Who have you helped clothe? Who have you fed?"
come the whispers, and "Who's empty now?" comes the taunt—
not from him, but from within myself:
it's that niggling conscience that points out every petty fault.

A food cart rolls by. I gaze at the sky.
Providence? Maybe yes. Maybe no. But I stop the questions.
I place my order at the cart, and then from heart and soul I offer
sweet alms: a cup of hot chocolate I carefully put into the hands
of the man with his back against a wall.

Southern Paradox

Third grade,
first day:
Two eight-year-old girls,
we held out arms—not to shake hands "hello,"
but to study skin shades
side by side, one Negro, one white.
("Don't call them 'colored,'" I'd been warned.
"They don't like that anymore.")
Eyes the color of cured tobacco
reflected back in eyes somewhere between
the shade of pine needles and Carolina skies;
two little noses smelled soap,
shampoo and new saddle-shoe leather—
times two; relieved smile met relieved smile.
"We're not so different,"
she said. I agreed.
"We're the same except for our skin."
(Later in the year, some confusion and debate:
Coloring self-portraits,
we realized that Crayola tan or Crayola brown was a better fit
than Crayola black for Negroes
who now preferred to be called "black,"
and we white children weren't Crayola white
either—but neither were we
Crayola pink or Crayola peach.)

The previous year
had been the teachers' year,
Mama among those to integrate—
she, a first-year teacher, assigned
to a high school with a resentful principal.
But of course he'd felt irate!

The powers that be had taken away
many of his best and blessed
the white schools with them and given him
unproven Caucasians—not exactly a fair exchange.
At my elementary school, we'd hardly
noticed; white or black, teachers were basically the same: mostly nice,
but anyone who wanted to stay all day in a classroom must be a bit
   odd. . . .

By junior high, I
found it easier to forget the differences,
the lines between black and white with no space for gray,
but for the ugly observations I still sometimes made—
like the time a boy brought a model KKK cross burning
for a project in our modern-history class (sort of like a model
volcano, except instead of play lava,
this one erupted in fake fire);
or when I learned
that my new school friend
had great-grandparents who'd once belonged
to the ancestors of another
friend whose family had helped found
our church. "Our people didn't know
any better," one Sunday-school teacher
excused all our Southern white ancestors
by way of explanation.
"Even Moses, in the Bible, was once a slave."
That was one Bible lesson
that didn't lift my spirits.

Dreaming without Feeling

I.

I've spent too many recent midnights open-eyed,
haunted by pernicious nightmares—past fears
of the bogeyman in my bedroom closet come to life
in darkness—while I watched patterns that moonlight made
through the slats of my window blinds: I need
rest, repose, deep rejuvenating sleep
so desperately—and so I determine
to practice dreaming without feeling.

II.

Some self-help article I read in a woman's magazine said
how we can train our minds, even while
supposedly unconscious, to fight toward awareness
enough that we can thought-stop and change our dreams;
the author advised, "Recognize them for what they are.
Tell yourself, 'I realize this is just a nightmare—
merely an unconscious drama—and I have the power to edit the
 script!'"
This is how to halt the fear: to dream without feeling.

III.

The cinnamonic crispness of wood smoke rises to my nostrils,
and the spearmint in his kiss lingers on my lips;
the scratchy classic elegance of a Billie Holliday LP sets the tone.
But suddenly it turns all wrong. He's not what I thought.
The scene transforms and my senses overwhelm
as twirling notes mutate into threats and screams,
and gentle sweetness becomes brute violence—scratches, punches,
 slaps—
and in the fire's flames I see a man-turned-demon.

IV.

I realize this is just a nightmare; in partial awareness,
I think: "I have the power to edit the script!"
Hollers for help: gone. Can't get Billie Holliday back either,
though—so I try to make the wind howl in my mind,
the kind of breeze that swirls fall leaves or bends spring-green trees
   in play.
Okay, good . . . Now I envision a lawn filled with whirligigs
spinning in that howling wind, the whirligig propellers painted
lavender, puce, magenta, the yard toys planted in grass on celadon
   sticks.

V.

I'm controlling and not reacting, seeing but not feeling—
as if I'd analyzed the scene in an impassive way
and decided to yell "Cut!" before I might anger my audience
with an obviously cheap attempt at emotional manipulation.
No longer an actor in my horror dreamscapes, I've become
screenwriter, producer and director extraordinaire.
I've put the magazine writer's advice into action, I register vaguely—
and then I roll over and pull my blankets tighter around me.

Lot's Wife, Revised and Updated for a New Millennium

I start down the stairs,
steep, same-colored treads
going all the way down, and
suddenly they drop into nothing—
nothing's there leading
into an abyss,
like a night-
mare I once had where a gaping maw
of sticky brick-red Carolina clay sucked
me into the ground, grasping at
my legs in a quicksand that wasn't sand
but earth of my native land.

I try to turn around,
so swivel my head with a sort of startled-
owl curiosity to see
if I can glimpse the other side,
if I have any hope of flight,
but what's above blurs into blindness
and my neck sticks as if
restrained in a brace—can't move beyond
a certain point. That point—
ah, yes, now reality hits—*that point*
proves the only certain thing
I know any more.

Farewell Father

> *In memory of S. P. and W. J.*
> *and in honor of their families who still miss them*

He said he couldn't stand to climb the heights
or bend his back to the work until he touched the depths
any more; no, no more
would he find the energy for living, only for existing—
his Paradise had been lost, never again to be regained.

A hero out of his beloved quest literature, he
prepared for his penultimate journey,
looking to travel lightly:
a bottle of the best eighty-
proof hooch and a prayer for mercy when the end came.

A man of faith and love, he
believed we'd forgive, felt sure we'd understand—
at least, that is what I like to think—
so he left no note,
only the loud obviousness of his absence.

Having arrived home, this time we knew we were alone
when all we heard was the hollow
silence in response
to our calling out his name—*hello*.
He had been home, but now he was gone.

At last he found rest beneath a tree,
drunken scotch bottle in hand, in the shelter of the winter woods;
he'd left his coat behind—he'd sought to shed layers,
and I hope he shed sadness
when the angels bore him away.

Springtime on Stage

Now that the snow has departed, my counselor,
my friend, that blue haze of which you spoke
has materialized while you waited, feet propped on desk,
watching old men on canes shuffling toward the fire hall for
their weekly poker game. It was not truly
blue, you said, or a game, but only
a perspective through which to watch a changing
tableau of actors backstage between scenes.

I fell asleep too easily, and woke fearful
that I may have missed the coming
of that blue fog that rises from the melting snow
and signals so much more. . . .
You were leading me out of a trance,
my mind still compartmentalized
into neat little, half-empty boxes
that echoed with the hum and underlying, regular clicks
of a tape recorder continuing to run; I could see
foothills far below and cities sprouting brick and concrete
atop dull asphalt, while, just outside your window,
it seemed gray, barren trees reached branches toward me
in supplication—but now, as I recount this, new buds begin
to force their way through once-frost-laden limbs.

Two months ago, I interpreted ink blots to your
satisfaction: This is a snow angel,
that an icicle, this other frost on a pine needle:
I was so obvious, you chuckled—obvious but sane.
And yet, now that the snow has departed, I wonder
if that blue haze will swallow us all into eternal obscurity. . . .

Practicing Therapy

Okay, I say, *okay—so this is how it is.*
Then I repeat back to you what you told me.
Is that correct? At your compliant nod, I ask,
And how does that make you feel?

I'm practicing, you see—practicing on you
what's previously been practiced on me:
It's been like a clinical circus
at times—three rings, each
with a freak show, and a barker (oops, therapist!)
narrating the scene as he or she sees it.

And I've learned—oh, how I've learned—
the "right" things to say and do,
even as my mind checks out and moves on
to whatever is most consuming me at the moment:

a flash of hummingbird wings blurring air outside
her window, the dizzying pattern on his tie
with all the shapes that almost illogically interconnect,
piles of laundry still to be put away,
not to mention what's for dinner tomorrow
and concern about the sirens I'm hearing on the streets here now—
these topics are the colons, semicolons, commas and em dashes
of my life, the momentary pauses between the parts;

it's caused by the fatigue of talking things through—
a tired jaw and the sense I've said it all before,
a fear of clichés and a motivation not to be labeled
as a sayer but not a doer. So I talk with you,
put into practice what I've learned, and pray that you won't look
away—at all the colons, semicolons, commas and em dashes of your life.

My Friend Persimmon

      My friend Persimmon
          was named so
              by her rough,
                  salty
                      mother
        because, she said, for the
            first
            time
                in her life,
                    she was dazzled by beauty.
        So sure was
            Persimmon's
                mother
        that she did
not
        shrink,
            or
      vault,
            or
snap
                under the pressure
                    of the
                ever-ensuing
laughter.
                Instead, she would
                    lift
                          her tiny frame
                in its usual tautness,
                    and
                wet her
                        ever-moist lips
                in reply.

Monkey Business

Hand over hand, across
the monkey bars, we climbed,
bodies dangling over dirt,
afraid to fall, yet pushing on
because an alternate did not exist.

Sometimes fifty feels the same as five,
when you find yourself
looking back, looking down, looking ahead,
and not wanting to leap,
forcing yourself to hang on and keep going.

Or will you swing your legs
over a rung, loop your knees around
it and gain a new perspective:
consider a different point of view
and turn the world as you know it on its head?

Revelation

Yeah, it's okay being
the posterior of an amoeba, shaking like a hula
dancer in the moss-green river water, &
even when the end comes (perhaps by drought
or through the explosion & conflagration of this earth),
when the end has proceeded beyond being
a far-future moment of apocalypse & the revelation
of a timeless time (it's called the future;
it's called now; it's called history; it's called
everything at once: hierarchy, survival of the fittest &
mutation), when all of that has come, & changed & gone,
then it still won't truly be over.

The extermination of my world will expand
the universe in one hundred-thousand different
ways; the echoing din of my demise
will invade empty space—I'll feel super-
naturally compelled to communicate that
there's a finish line here, even though it looks
as infinitely plummeting as a luge-runner's tunnel
of curving ice, & you'll see
that finish line in a satellite continuing to spin
or in a falling star that burns out before it can find
any place to hit down; like an empty glove,
the blackness will be there to be filled,
& you won't be able to see beyond,
but you'll still hear my music—
the tune of the moss-green river-water hula—
that tells of life stories & other histories—
if you will only stop & listen.

The Radiant Point

Golden shimmer sizzles
a descending demise
a path through pallid predawn sky
a flaming heavenly messenger
searing the earthly world

Ash-hot coal touched to grass as if in
silencing rebuke
creates a cloud of steam
against crackling silver hoarfrost
upon pastures where stars rain down

Wordless supplications breathe a late-December fog
that hangs in our automobile's interior
before it dissipates along with those voiceless prayers
those meditations examining the heart
searching within the soul for confession and forgiveness

Spirit reflects light and flame and fire
a meteoric minister from
a celestial radiant point
shining like a falling star
yet hopeful of redemption before it utterly burns out

The Prospect (Park) of a Perfect Summer Day

We strolled along Nostrand,
we four, from our
Queens-based A train
to the hills of Brooklyn's Crown Heights, to Eastern Parkway,
which looked incredibly broad and impossibly green
on this spring-cool summer day—nothing like Labor Day
when it's overtaken by steel bands, Carnival bands,
soca songs blaring from flatbed trucks, and
politicians parading and stopping to be seen eating curry.

By the Brooklyn Museum, my husband remarked that
it's no Met, and it's no MOMA, and it's no Guggenheim—
and it's in an outer borough . . .
not a condemnation, but simply an observation
of Manhattanites' sentiments;
we in the so-called outer boroughs
so often feel our own New York City neighborhoods
regarded as forgotten stepchildren
to incomparable Manhattan.

But, on this day, Brooklyn was our desired destination,
Prospect Park our anticipated goal. And when we got there, we kept
    walking—
by botanical garden flowers in contained displays,
by animals caged in houses in the little zoo,
by a little girl learning to ride on a bike path, and
by a boathouse beside electric-green-algae-filled water,
on paved paths, on gravel tracks,
beside waterfalls, and through tunnels
that echoed the *hello, hello*'s of our tuneless quartet.

Statues rose, stony and gray-green
in the distance, and we read
metal poles topped with informational markers:
The Battle of Long Island was fought here.
General Sullivan's army marched through this area.
Emerging near fields filled with dandelion weeds, we followed
asphalt paths between knolls populated with running children,
and a boy trying to bat the balls his father tossed, and a baby
sunning on a blanket between picnicking parents.

And then we climbed a set of stairs,
and passed through a gate, and just like that we'd left behind
the prospect of a perfect summer day.

Reunion

Sitting over coffee amidst the crumbs of our shared discourse,
our smiles now thinning and strained
after four courses over several hours,
we're surrounded by plates puddled with olive oil,
stray strands of linguine and a sandy dusting of parmesan,
worn out from our efforts to celebrate
the way we think we ought. Is this what comes
of old-fashioned social networking—face-to-face?
We'd imagined the perfect presentation:
the pretty dresses, the handsome suits, the witty toasts prompting
white-toothed half smiles to be captured on camera-phones;
but none of us is alone here—the sole focus of it all—
this is family-style dining, secular communion,
a visitation that brought us here together.
A little something sweet to finish—this is what we crave:
tartufo, tiramisu, demitasses of espresso
to add strength to the sweetness,
to lend credence to the sense
that not all that's saccharine
has a palatable taste without some contrast to counter it.
Before we stand to go our separate ways,
we put away our portable devices
to leave a tip: no more posing for now—for these last moments
we'll simply enjoy being our real selves together.

Reflections

These are my rivers, these my lakes;
I view them as through a bronze mirror,
creating poetry in the obscure as much as in the clear—
the mercy of this is in the perspective:
rose, dagger, face, fear . . . or simply water, depending upon
    appearance.

These are my rivers, these my oceans;
bird by bird soars over them, while fish by fish glides within,
and I, who once thought I had a heart of the wilderness,
find myself lost between that above and that beneath, between men
    and angels,
between a place where angels fall and one where more than the last
    good man yet lives.

The Other Side

The Danish say the soul needs an open window
through which to escape to the sky; it would go
away from the bed in the master suite
where the body alone remains.
Near the headboard, there's a chair
where a new widower sits, flesh and spirit still intact.
He speaks to a doctor standing in the doorway—
the husband talks of timing medicines and making notes
of physical reactions and developing symptoms,
then segues into an explanation
of his pocket-watch collection
(of how this one opens at the twelve,
that one at the nine, and
of how you can view the movement through the back
of this other), while in the meantime
his wife's soul soars on the breeze.

A lamp, a glass of water, and bottles of pills
crowd the top of a bedside table,
and he observes the turn of the table's spindle legs;
he tries to focus on breathing, but hears
the Vivaldi he's left playing in the background—
almost vulgar the way it intrudes.
Why can't he concentrate on what he should—
or on whom? The physician has come in—
when?—written on some papers and forms, and
moves now to pull the sheet over the corpse's face.
The corpse! thinks the survivor. The corpse: his wife!
"She's gone," says the doctor as
if the patient's husband didn't know.
It's the book-smart man who doesn't know,
though, thinks the husband—because, just on the other side,
his wife's spirit is flying free.

Additional Acknowledgments

Thanks also go out to those people who have taught, critiqued, supported and encouraged me throughout the years; in no particular order, these include Nancy Banks and the late Muriel Waters Allison for encouraging my love of writing when I was their student; Hollins University professors and writers R. H. W. Dillard and Jeanne Larsen, who have remained friends and mentors to me for many years; poets Ardis Kimzey and Betty Adcock, whose workshops inspired me during my early years of poetry writing; Finishing Line Press editors Christen Kincaid and Leah Maines for seeing something special in *Borderlands* and guiding it through the publication process; and my family—particularly my parents, Philip and Mary Alice Blank; my parents-in-law, Keith and Marian Birth; and extra-special thanks to my husband, Kevin Birth, and to our sons, Brendan and Aidan.

Margaret Adams Birth has been widely published, both in the U.S. and abroad. Her poetry has appeared in journals ranging from *White Wall Review* (Canada), to *The New Voices* (Trinidad and Tobago), to *Purple Patch* (England), to *Perceptions* (her poem "Jane Doe," published there in 1993, a Pushcart Prize nominee). Her "sweet" secular and Christian fiction, mostly written as Maggie Adams, includes a multicultural romance novelette, *Bride at First Sight* (Boroughs Publishing, 2013) and over two dozen anonymously penned stories for confession magazines (*True Confessions*, etc.). Her mystery stories, which she pens as Rhett Shepard, have appeared in *Kings River Life Magazine* and in the anthology *The Killer Wore Cranberry: Room for Thirds* (Untreed Reads, 2013). She also spent over a decade working as a freelance manuscript reader, proofreader and copy editor for several major publishers. Raised in North Carolina, and educated at Hollins University and at the University of Rochester, from which she graduated with majors in anthropology, Spanish and English, she now lives in New York City with her family. She is a member of the Secular Franciscan Order and is a semi-professional genealogist. Her author page is at www.facebook.com/MaggieAdamsRhettShepard.

www.ingramcontent.com/pod-product-compliance
Lightning Source LLC
Chambersburg PA
CBHW051705040426
42446CB00009B/1318